The Art of

WORLD OF WARCRAFT

WRATH of the LICH KING

INSIGHT ◉ EDITIONS

San Rafael, California

INSIGHT ◉ EDITIONS
17 Paul Drive : San Rafael : CA : 94903
phone 415.526.1370 • fax 415.526.1394
www.insighteditions.com

Printed in Canada by Palace Press International
www.palacepress.com

Contents

Foreword 10

Rise of the Lich King 12

Death Knights 28

Howling Fjord 44

Borean Tundra 68

Dragonblight 82

Grizzly Hills 94

Zul'Drak 104

Sholazar Basin 112

Crystalsong Forest 120

Storm Peaks 130

Icecrown 138

Sindragosa 172

Black Temple 182

The Gods of Zul'Aman 186

Fury of the Sunwell 190

Phat Lewtz 194

Colophon 208

Foreword

Here's what I would LOVE to be able to say: the fantastic art you are about to witness is a direct result of my personal brilliance.

I would love to be able to take a big chunk of the credit, soak up the limelight, and reap the subsequent rewards. I would love to be able to do that, but in lieu of making this piece an exercise in self-indulgence, I suppose the truth will have to suffice. And the truth is deceptively simple. But we'll get to that in a minute. Let's save the best for last. First, let's talk about some of the challenges the Art Team faced on WotLK....

To begin with, there was the challenge of shifting from the far-flung high fantasy of the Burning Crusade to a more traditional gothic fantasy style and somehow keeping it all fresh.

Then there was the challenge of navigating the various pitfalls of an established game with established lore, an established style, and an engine that, while dependable and efficient, can be more than a little stubborn.

There have been numerous other challenges as well, but you get the idea. *So, you may ask, how does one overcome such hurdles?* What sage advice can I offer? What pearls of wisdom can I impart? As I said, the truth is simple. To get results from a team of artists like the ones I work with, I suggest you do one thing:

Stay out of their way.

Sure, you may need to ensure that their works are in keeping with the style, lore, etc. of the Warcraft universe, but beyond that, the smartest thing to do is to let them work their magic. If you do that, the results will speak for themselves.

And that, my friends, is the simple truth.

I hope you enjoy looking at this art as much as we enjoyed making it. The WoW Art Team is full of artists who are passionate about the game and the art they make for it. This book is a testament to their hard work and love for their craft.

Thank you, and enjoy!

– Chris G. Robinson

Rise of the Lich King

THREATENED WITH ETERNAL TORMENT, the orc shaman Ner'zhul swore to serve the demonic Burning Legion, and so the demon lord Kil'jaeden transformed Ner'zhul into the Lich King. Wary of betrayal, Kil'jaeden trapped Ner'zhul's spirit in a suit of armor, bound the captive spirit to the runeblade Frostmourne, and sealed both armor and blade within a specially crafted block of ice. Kil'jaeden cast this crystal into the world of Azeroth. The frozen cask, warped by its violent descent, had come to resemble a throne when it landed in the snowy wastes of Northrend.

At Kil'jaeden's command, Ner'zhul created a plague of undeath designed to eradicate humanity. He also secretly pushed Frostmourne out of the Frozen Throne. He intended for the sword to lure a champion who would become a vessel for Ner'zhul's restless spirit....

When the plague began affecting Lordaeron, the sorceress Jaina Proudmoore and the king's only son, Prince Arthas Menethil, investigated its origin. They found that the plague was spreading via infected grain. They also discovered that the plague's victims would arise as murderous undead agents of an army called the Scourge.

Prince Arthas grew obsessed with destroying the Scourge. Alienating Jaina with his increasingly ruthless tactics, Arthas tracked the source of the plague to Northrend. There his quest led him to Frostmourne, and although an inscription warned that Frostmourne's power came at a terrible cost, the prince took up the sword and forfeited his soul.

Returning to Lordaeron, Arthas killed his father and nearly annihilated the entire high elf race. After the Third War, however, the Lich King began to weaken, and the Frozen Throne came under attack. Hastily Arthas returned to Northrend and vanquished the attackers. He then shattered the Frozen Throne and donned Ner'zhul's helm, sealing his union with the Lich King at last.

Glenn Rane '07

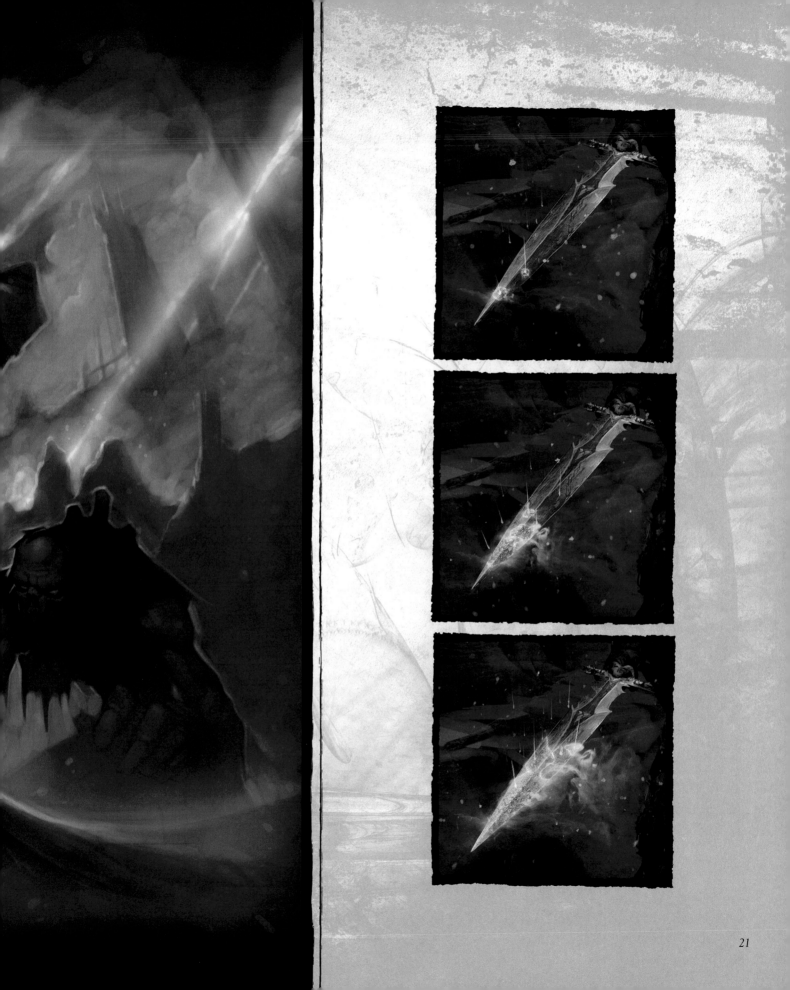

Death Knights

D EATH KNIGHTS ARE HIGHLY POWERFUL, malevolent, runeblade-wielding warriors of the Scourge. The first and greatest of them was Prince Arthas.

In recent years the power and fury of the death knights have only grown. Now these unrelenting crusaders of the damned eagerly await the Lich King's command to unleash their fury on Azeroth once again.

Glenn Rane

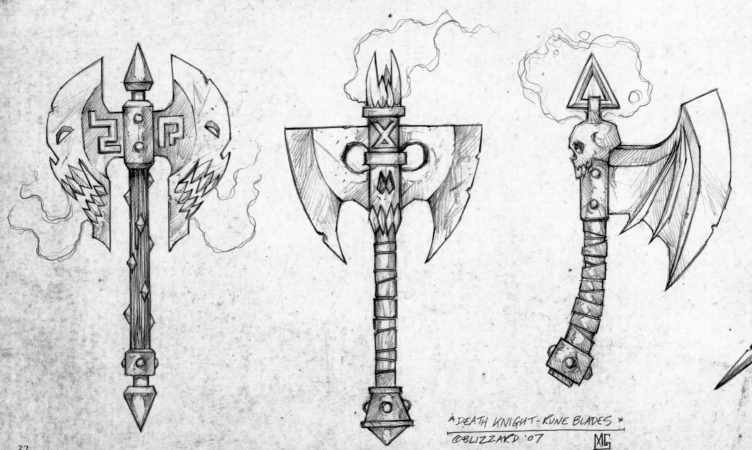

DEATH KNIGHT-RUNE BLADES
@BLIZZARD '07

DEATH KNIGHT *
BLIZZARD '07

GLOWING RUNE
POMMEL

BLINKING
RED EYE OF
HILT

SMOKE
'TONGUE

GLENN RANE

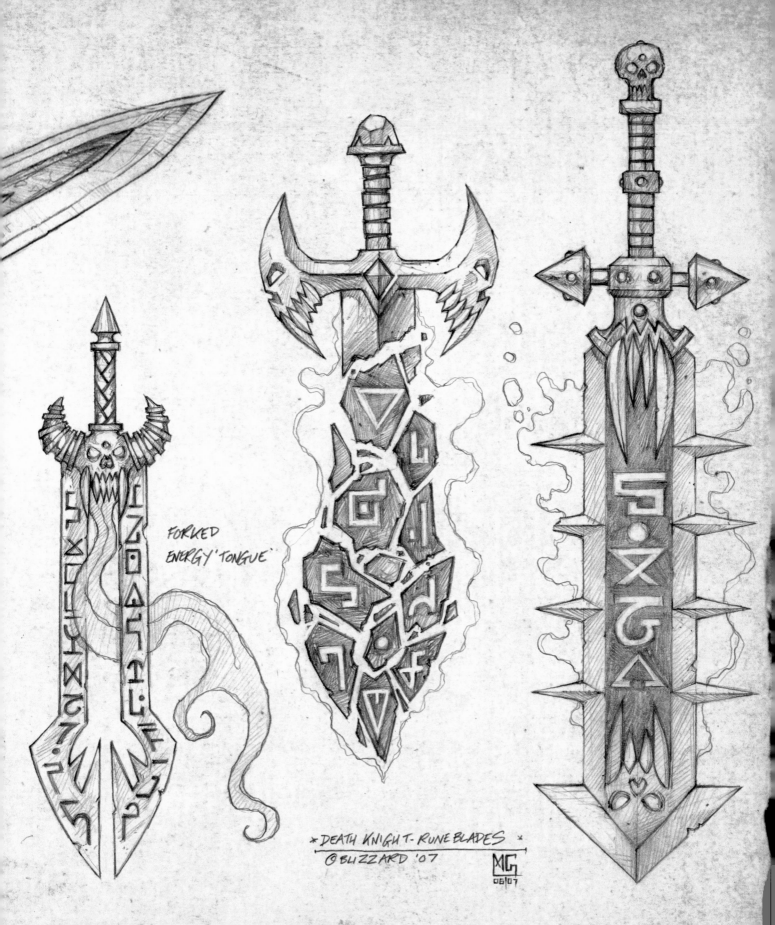

FORKED
ENERGY "TONGUE"

* DEATH KNIGHT · RUNE BLADES *
© BLIZZARD '07
MG
06/07

GlennRane '07

38 ∗ FEMALE BLOODELF DEATH KNIGHT ∗
    ⓒBLIZZARD '07

SHIELDS *
MG
07-07

* DWARF DEATH KNIGHT *

39

GlennRane 07

NIGHT-ELF DEATH KNIGHT

GLENN RANE 07
ORC DEATH KNIGHT

Howling Fjord

LONG AGO, BARBARIC, half-giant warriors called vrykul founded a vast civilization among the towering cliffs of the Howling Fjord. The vrykul prospered for many years, then vanished suddenly.

Now, awakened by some unknown force, the savage warriors have re-emerged to wage a brutal campaign of destruction from their stygian fortress of Utgarde Keep.

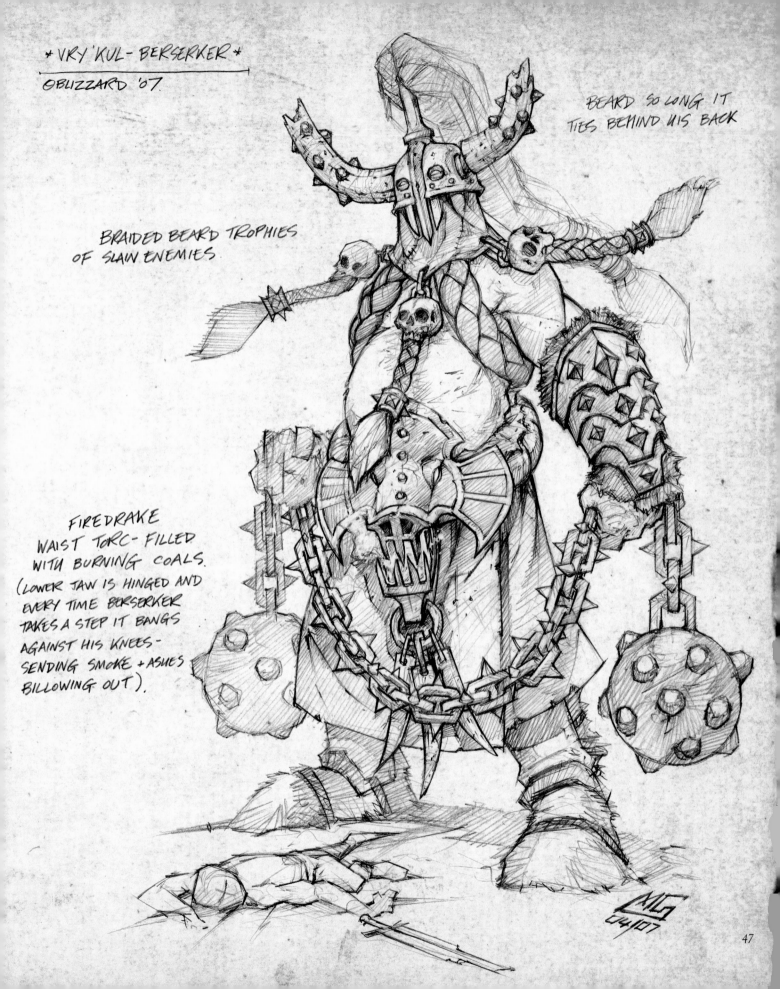

* VRY'KUL - BERSERKER *
©BLIZZARD '07.

BEARD SO LONG IT
TIES BEHIND HIS BACK

BRAIDED BEARD TROPHIES
OF SLAIN ENEMIES.

FIREDRAKE
WAIST TORC - FILLED
WITH BURNING COALS.
(LOWER JAW IS HINGED AND
EVERY TIME BERSERKER
TAKES A STEP IT BANGS
AGAINST HIS KNEES -
SENDING SMOKE + ASHES
BILLOWING OUT).

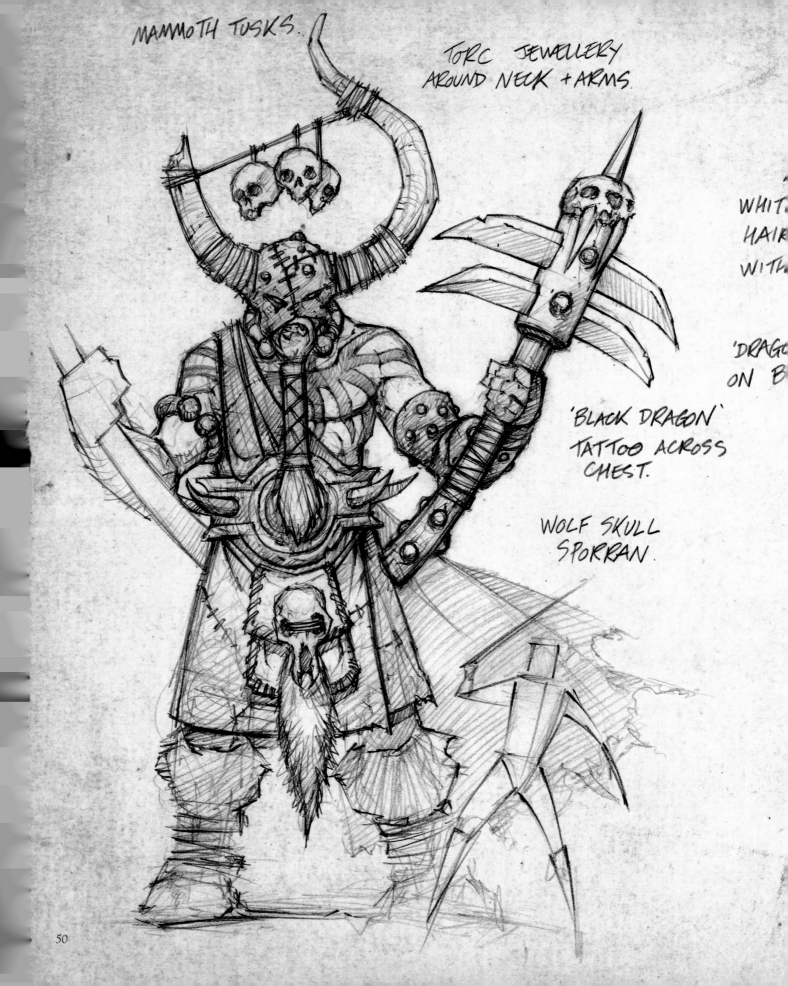

MAMMOTH TUSKS.

TORC JEWELLERY
AROUND NECK + ARMS.

WHIT
HAIR
WITH

'DRAGO
ON B

'BLACK DRAGON'
TATTOO ACROSS
CHEST.

WOLF SKULL
SPORRAN.

50

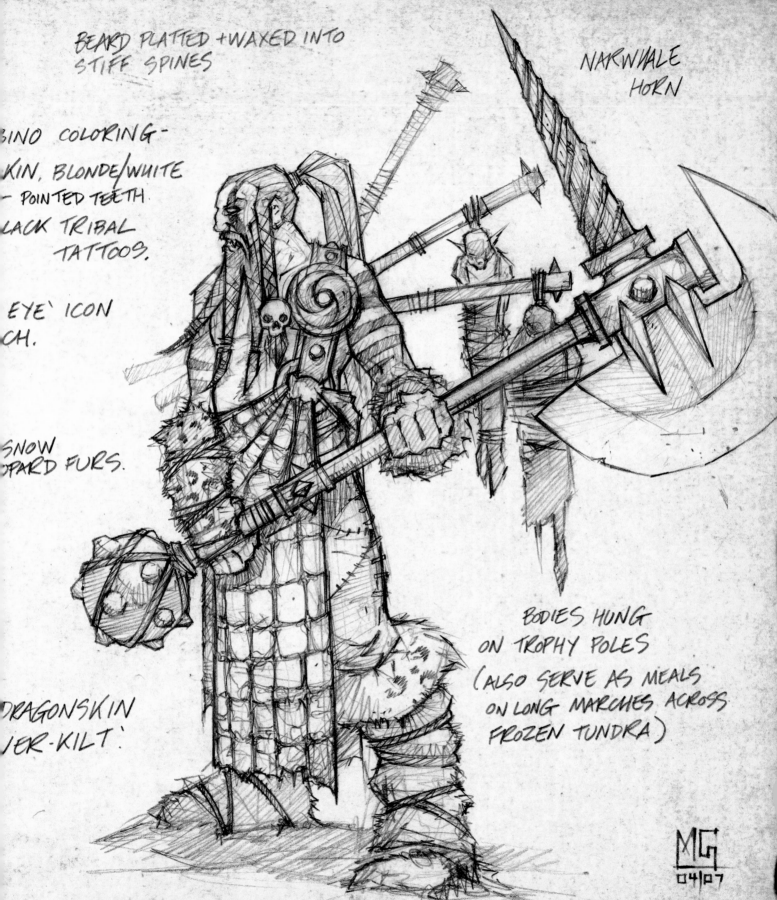

BEARD PLATTED + WAXED INTO
STIFF SPINES

NARWHALE
HORN

BINO COLORING-
KIN, BLONDE/WHITE
— POINTED TEETH
LACK TRIBAL
TATTOOS.

EYE` ICON
CH.

SNOW
PARD FURS.

BODIES HUNG
ON TROPHY POLES
(ALSO SERVE AS MEALS
ON LONG MARCHES ACROSS
FROZEN TUNDRA)

DRAGONSKIN
JER-KILT`

MG
04|07

51

Vry'kul
Dragon Witch

J. Kuna
4.07

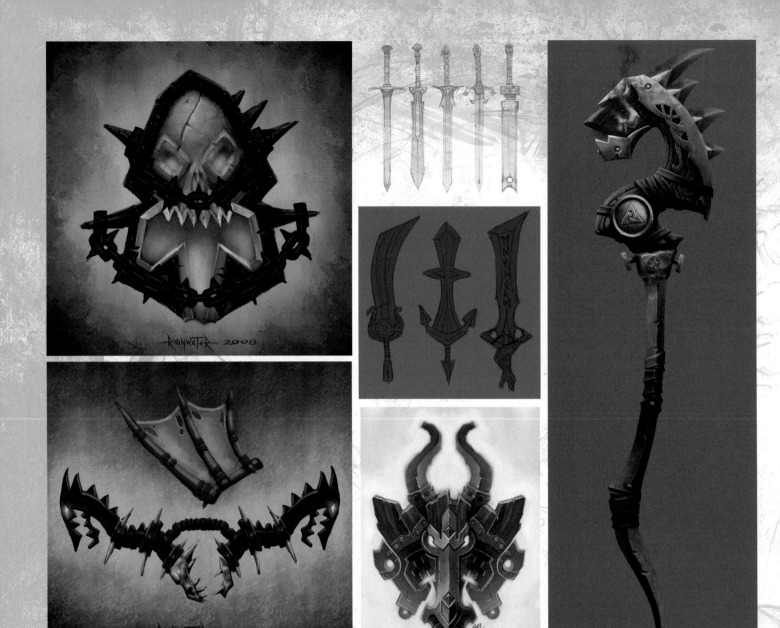

RAINWATER 2008

RAINWATER 2008

Borean Tundra

THE SPRAWLING BOREAN TUNDRA is home to both the walrus-like tuskarr and the enigmatic taunka. Here also, deep within the mountainous Coldarra, the blue Dragon Aspect, Malygos, has awakened and resumed his guardianship of all magic. Commanding the blue dragonflight from his mystical base, the Nexus, Malygos is determined to seize control of magic throughout the world.

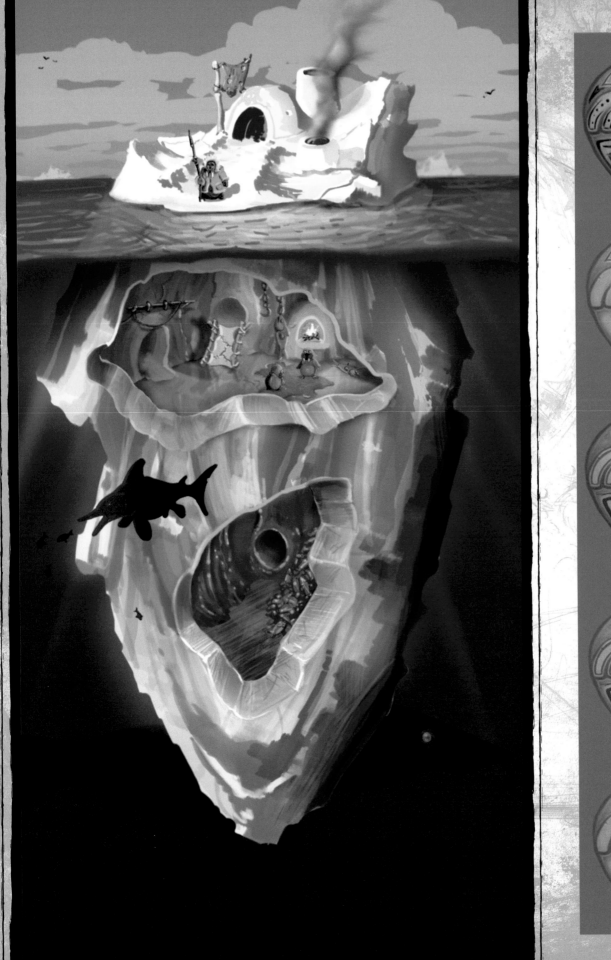

Glenn Rane

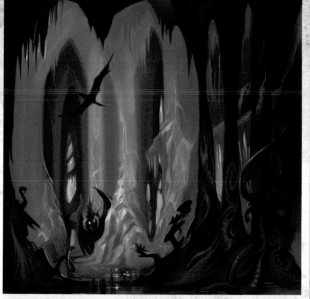

Dragonblight

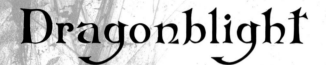

WITHIN THE DRAGONBLIGHT, the one-time seat of the nerubian empire, dense forests surround an arctic wasteland littered with the massive bones of dragons who came here to die. Here also resides the Chamber of the Aspects, where the five great Dragon Aspects were given their charge to watch over the newly created world of Azeroth.

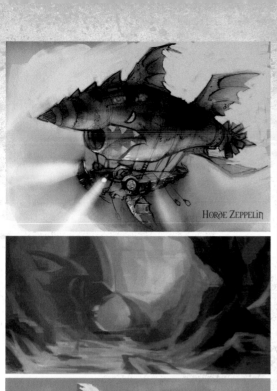

HORDE ZEPPELIN

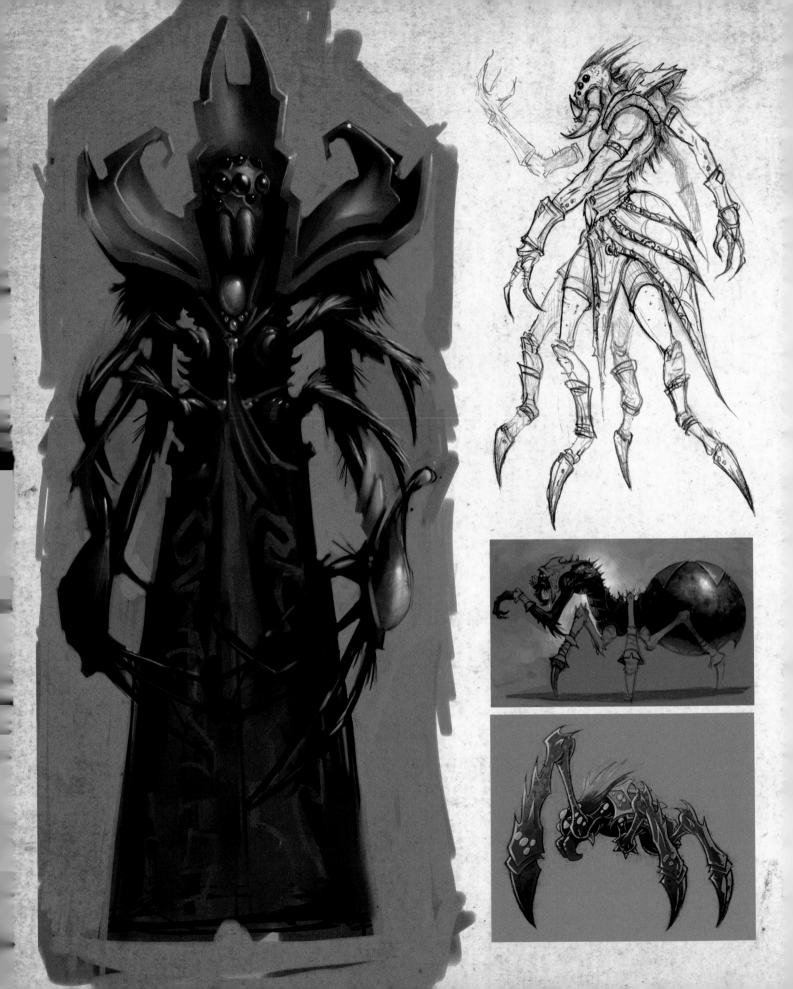

Grizzly Hills

IN THE HEART of this primordial frontier lies the ancestral home of the furbolgs, Grizzlemaw. Although plagued by trappers and the deforestation efforts of the goblin Venture Company, the furbolgs' most imminent threat comes from the north, where undead Drakkari ice trolls have begun pouring from their stronghold of Drak'Tharon Keep.

QUEEN

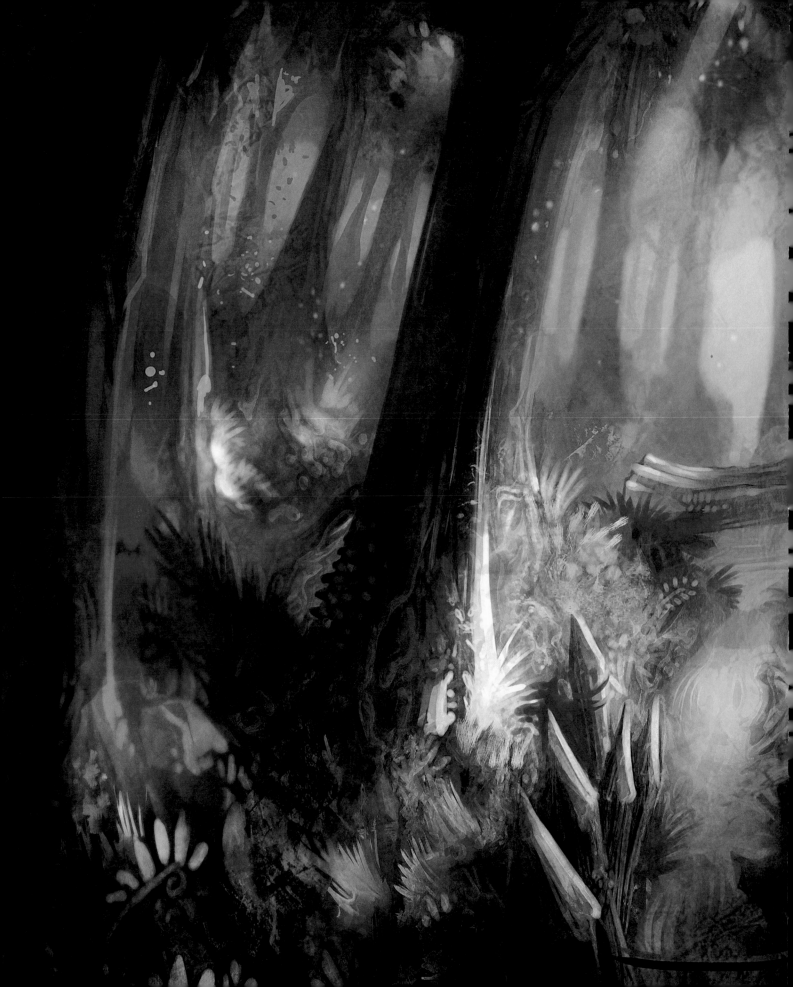

DEVIL-TREANT.
ZARD '07

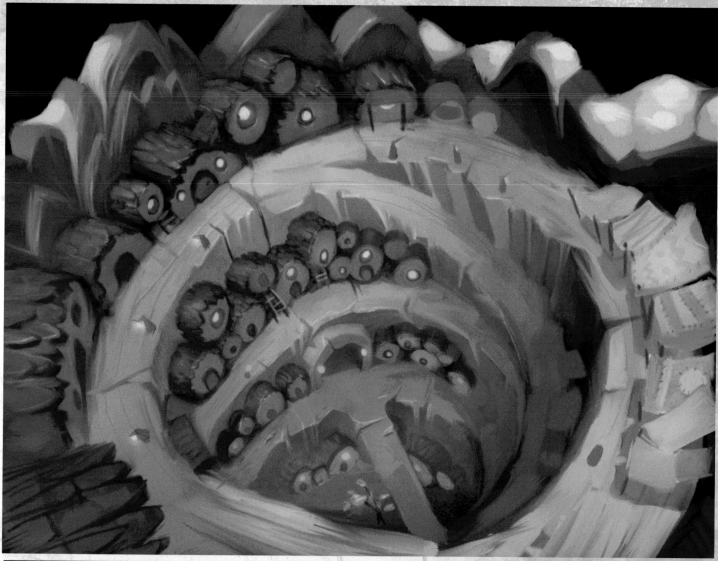

Zul'Drak

THE VICIOUS DRAKKARI ice trolls have carved out an existence in one of the most inhospitable climates on Azeroth. From their isolated base of Zul'Drak, the trolls are rumored to sacrifice captured animal gods and somehow siphon their untold powers, perhaps in preparation for the apocalypse they believe to be close at hand.

Sholazar Basin

SHOLAZAR BASIN is a self-contained environment where the world-shaping titans allowed their creations to roam and flourish. Shielded from the Scourge by a powerful magical barrier, the basin has remained a haven from the undead. It is viewed by many of Northrend's embattled races as a kind of promised land.

GLENN RANE 09

Crystalsong Forest

BEFORE THE SUNDERING, Highborne night elves lived in Crystalsong Forest and protected its trees with powerful sorcery. Today blood elves and high elves fight over the Highborne ruins. The forest is also the frontline in the battle between the blue dragon-flight and the Kirin Tor, who recently relocated their city of Dalaran to float above Crystalsong.

1

2

3

Storm Peaks

LEGENDS MAINTAIN that the benevolent titans monitored Azeroth from the Storm Peaks in the years following their reshaping of the world. It is further believed that the secrets of Azeroth's past, present, and future may be found inhe time-lost ruins of Ulduar.

STOVEPIPE HAT (LITERALLY!)

DRAGON HIDE CLOAK

MOUSTACHE TIPPED WITH BURNING PITCH

SMELTING POT BELT BUCKLE

SHIELD TOE-CAPS

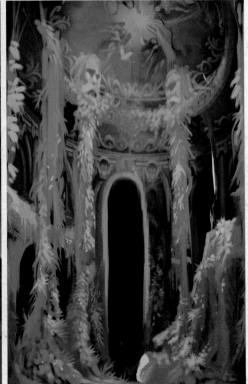

* ICE GIANT *
© BLIZZARD '07

SHIELD
SKIRT

...N JAW
...AIL

MITTENS WITH
SHIELD KNUCKLE-DUSTERS

OLD PORTCULLIS

SWORDS STRAPPED TO FEET -
ACTING AS CRAMPONS ON
ICY GROUND

137

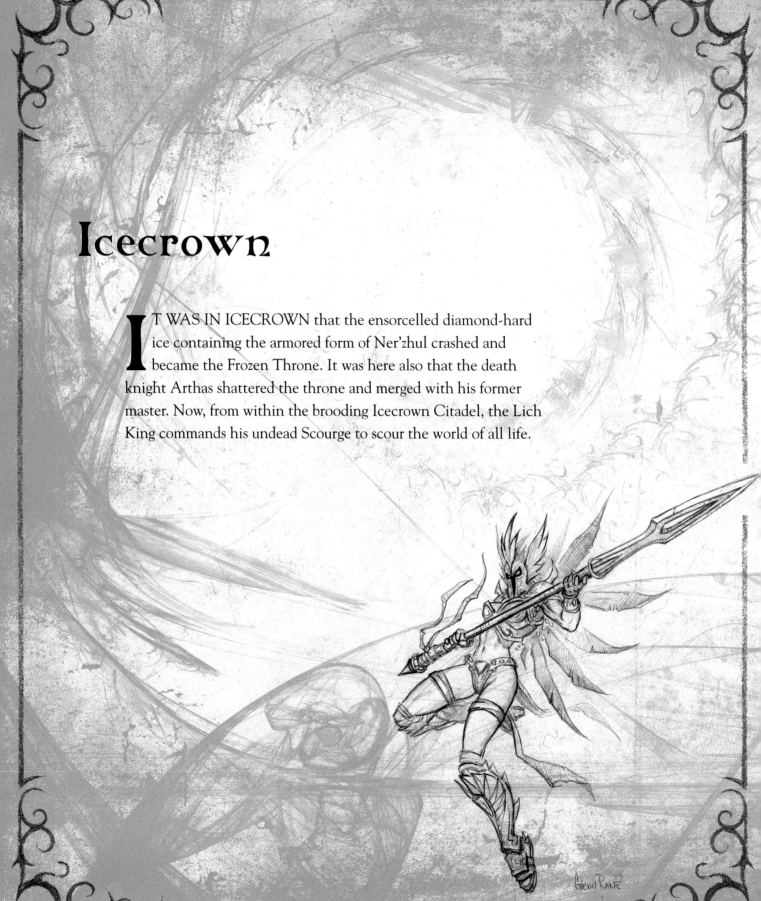

Icecrown

IT WAS IN ICECROWN that the ensorcelled diamond-hard ice containing the armored form of Ner'zhul crashed and became the Frozen Throne. It was here also that the death knight Arthas shattered the throne and merged with his former master. Now, from within the brooding Icecrown Citadel, the Lich King commands his undead Scourge to scour the world of all life.

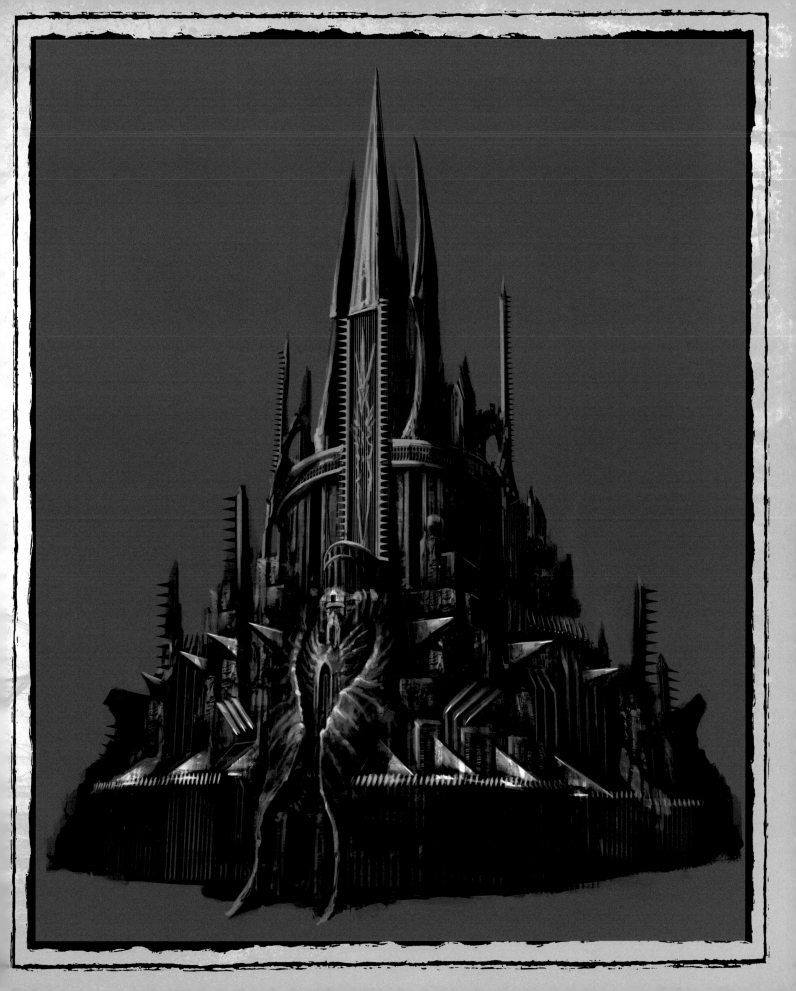

UNDEAD
FOREGROUND

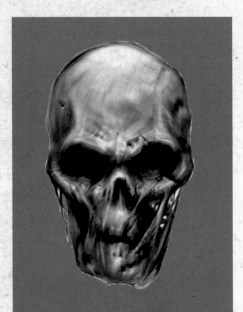

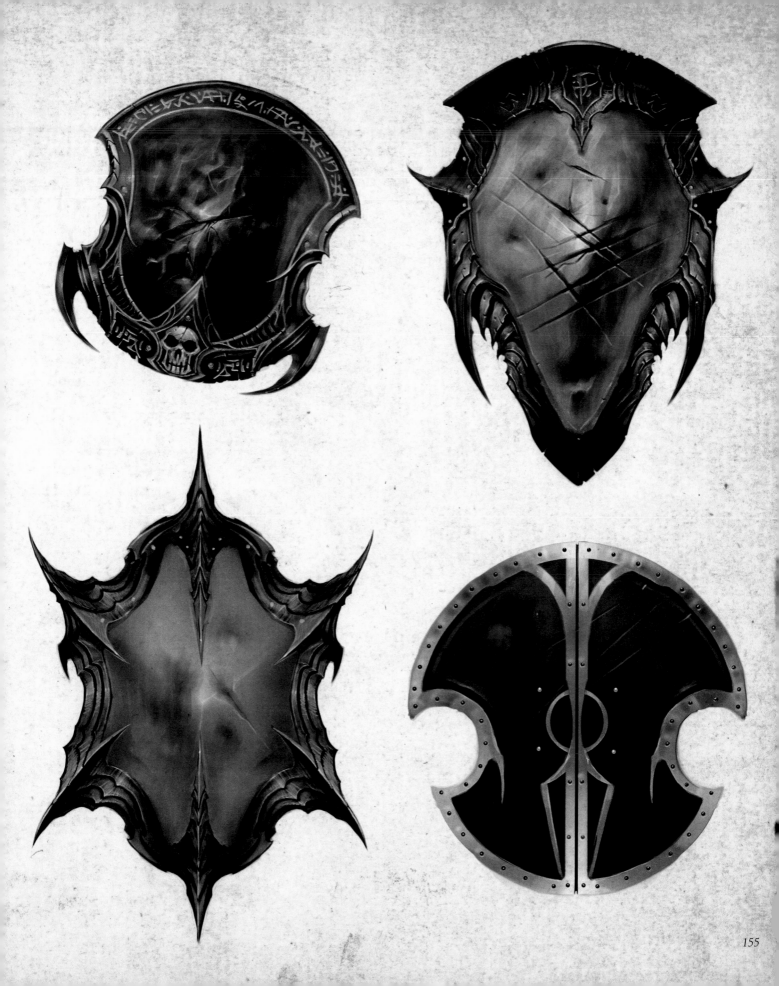

SHIELDS
+
WEAPONS RACK

Sindragosa, the Frost Queen

THE BLUE DRAGON ASPECT, Malygos, is the guardian of arcane magic. The bones of his first consort, Sindragosa, lay in the icy wastes of Northrend until the Lich King raised the skeleton into undeath. Now Sindragosa serves the Lich King as a frost wyrm, and the full measure of her dark, devastating power is only beginning to be realized.

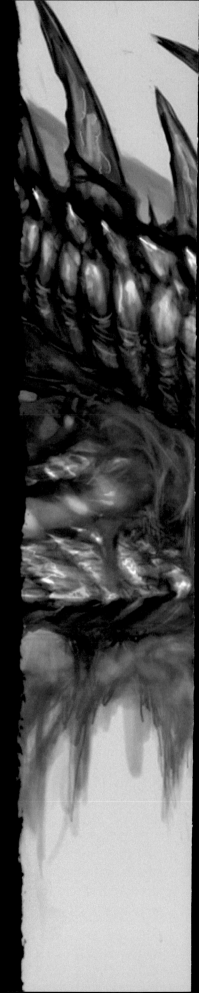

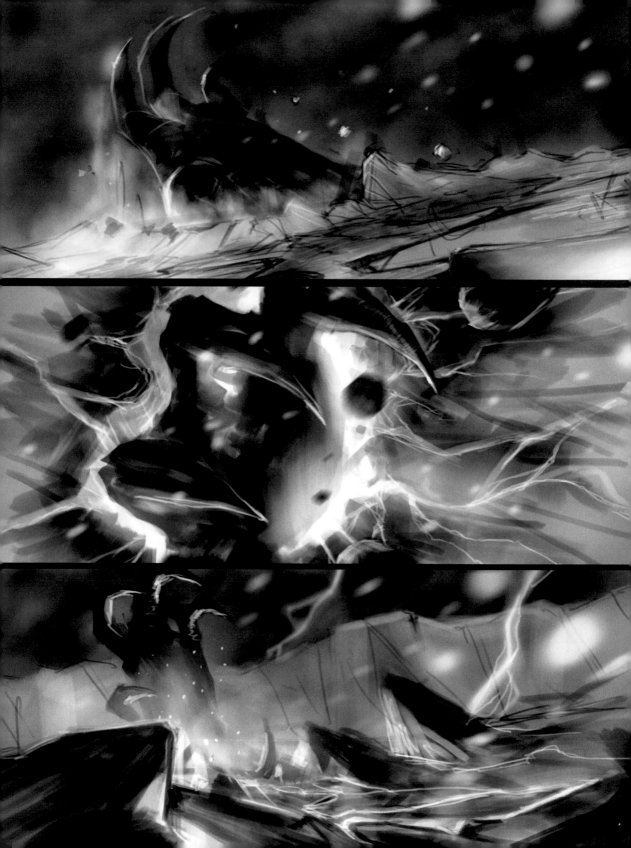

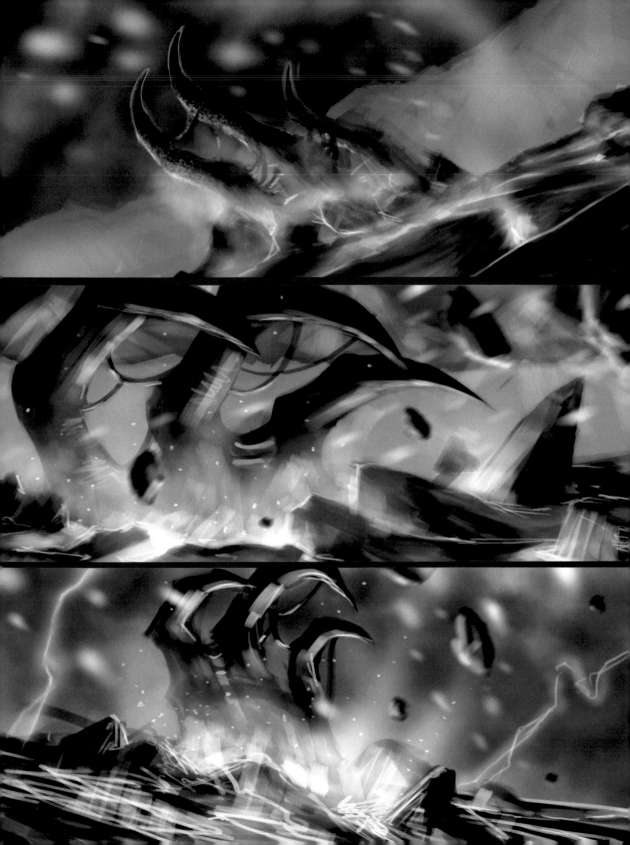

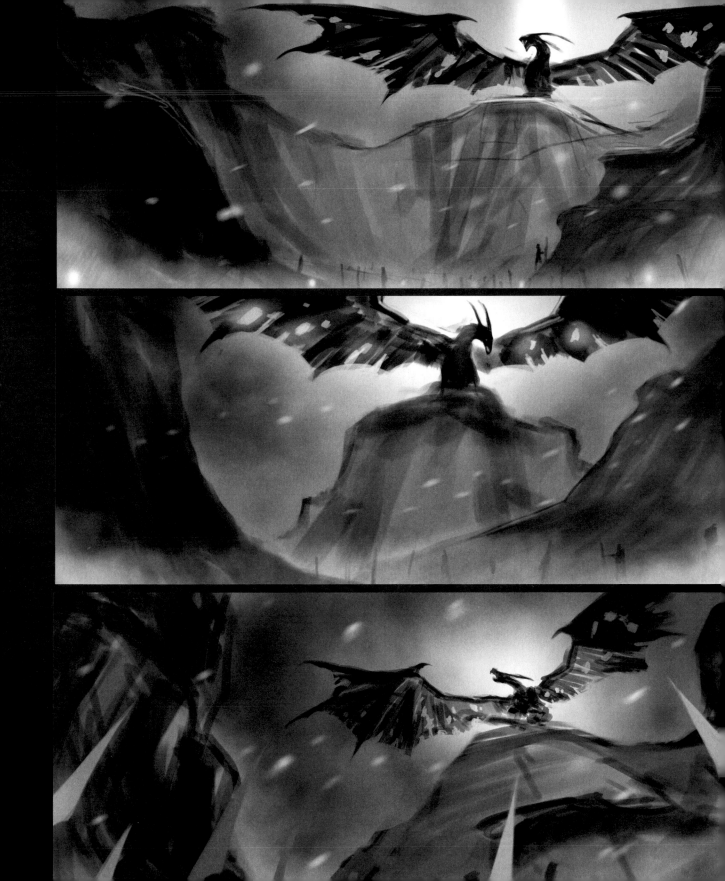

BLACK TEMPLE

Patch 2.1.0

THE TEMPLE of Karabor was a peaceful center of draenei worship until corrupted orcs seized the holy site. Known afterward as the Black Temple, the structure was occupied by the pit lord Magtheridon, who eventually fell to Illidan the Betrayer.

With Illidan defeated, the question remains: will the temple ever regain its former glory?

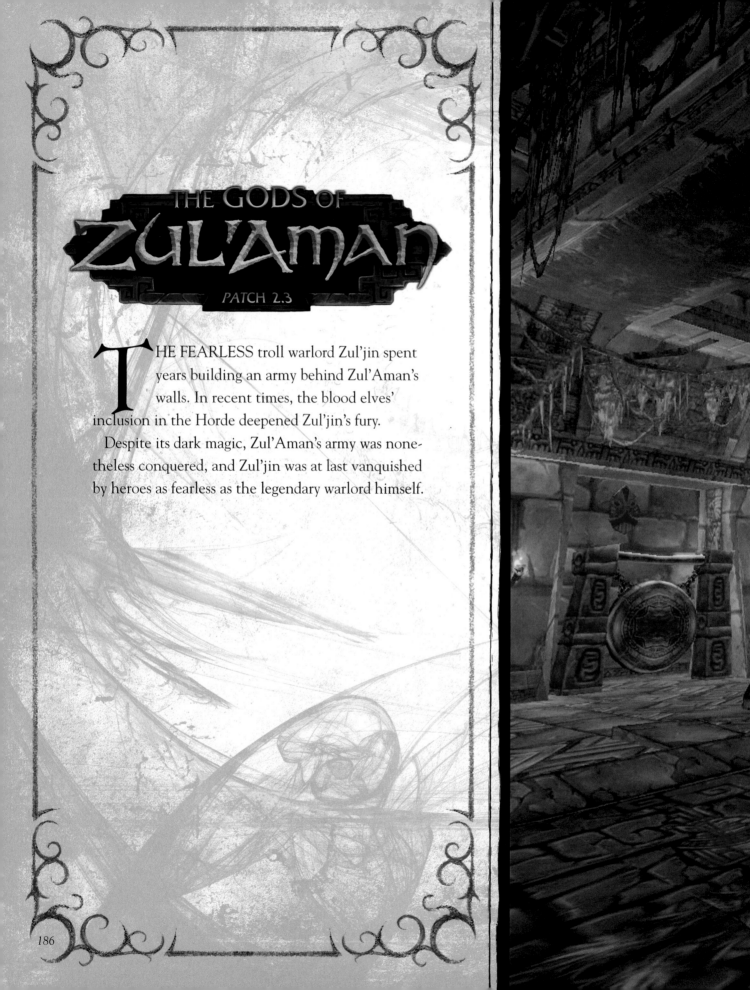

THE GODS OF ZUL'AMAN

PATCH 2.3

THE FEARLESS troll warlord Zul'jin spent years building an army behind Zul'Aman's walls. In recent times, the blood elves' inclusion in the Horde deepened Zul'jin's fury.

Despite its dark magic, Zul'Aman's army was nonetheless conquered, and Zul'jin was at last vanquished by heroes as fearless as the legendary warlord himself.

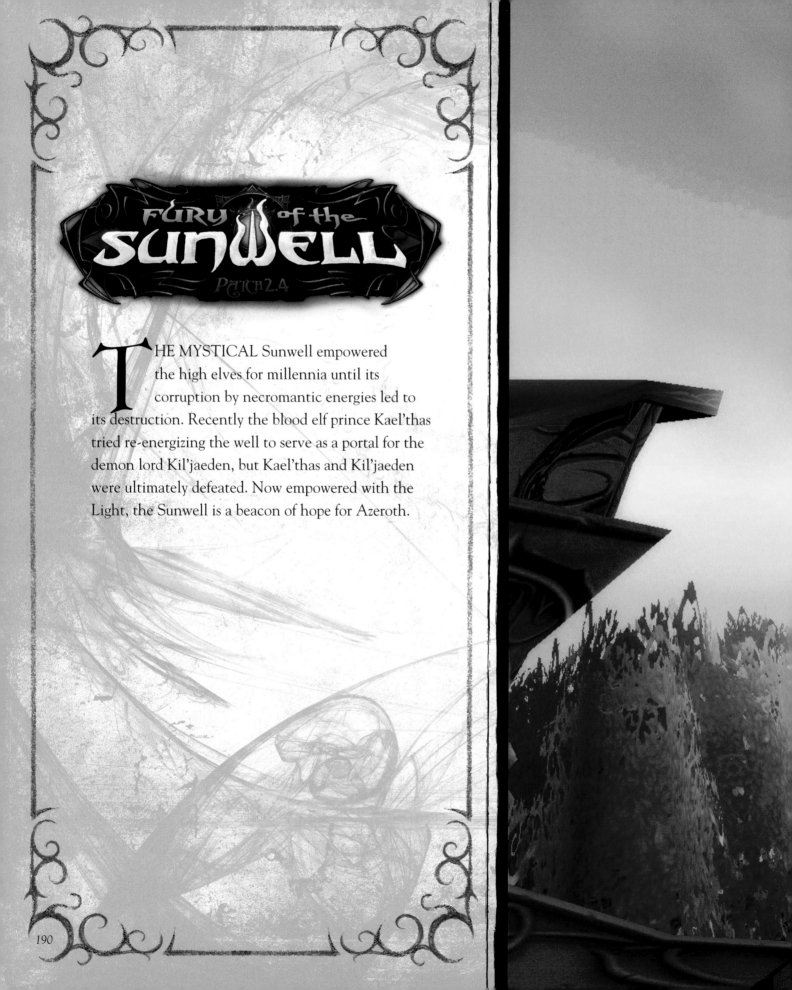

FURY of the SUNWELL
Patch 2.4

THE MYSTICAL Sunwell empowered the high elves for millennia until its corruption by necromantic energies led to its destruction. Recently the blood elf prince Kael'thas tried re-energizing the well to serve as a portal for the demon lord Kil'jaeden, but Kael'thas and Kil'jaeden were ultimately defeated. Now empowered with the Light, the Sunwell is a beacon of hope for Azeroth.

Phat Lewtz

What do you do with great pieces of art that don't fit neatly into a specific section? Create a bonus section, of course! Enjoy!

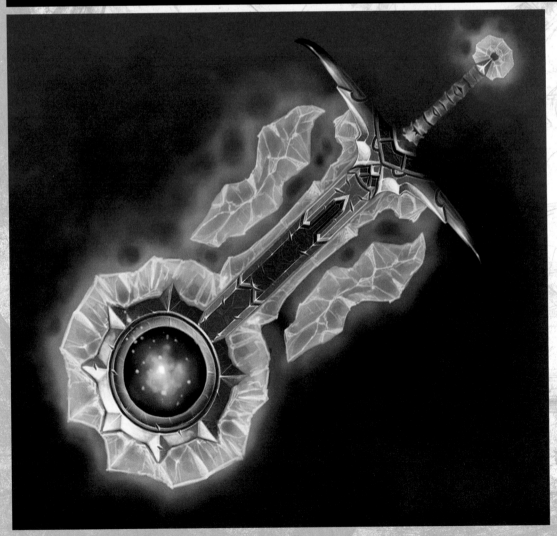

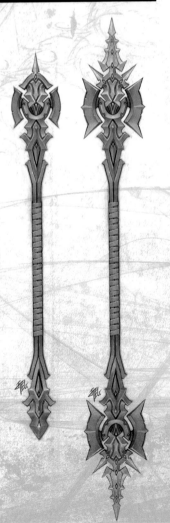

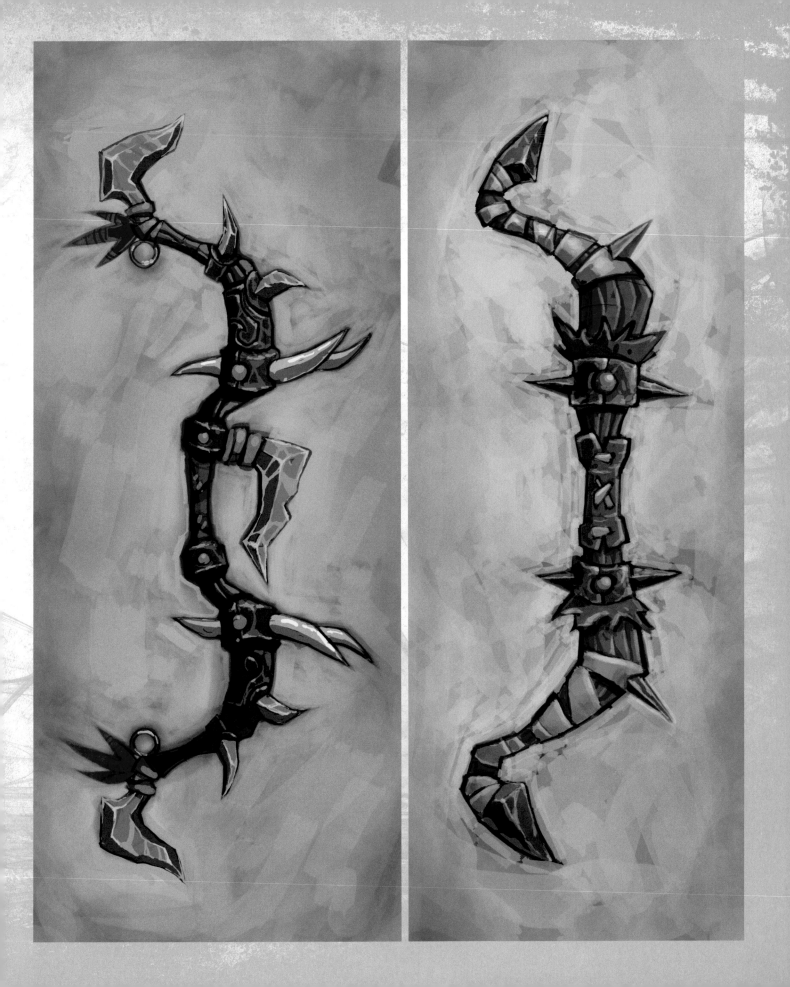

Colophon

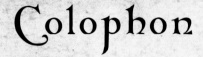

GAME ARTISTS
Steve Aguilar
Steve Allen
Blue
Sarah Boulian
Eric Browning
John Butkus
Ely Cannon
Jim Chadwick
Jamie Chang
Jeff Chang
Carman Cheung
Victor Chong
Steve Crow
Terrie Denman
Brett Dixon
Jonathan Dumont
Slim Ghariani
Mark Gibbons
Rutherford Gong
Jeremy Graves
Jeff Gregory
Kevin K Griffith
Chris Ha
Ed Hanes
Mauricio Hoffman
Mai Igarashi
Jonathan Jelinek
Trent Kanigua
Aaron Keller
Roman Kenney
Justin Kunz
Hun Lee
Peter Lee
Jimmy Lo
Chris Luckenbach
Kevin Maginnis
Andrew Matthews
Jon McConnell

Jesse McCree
Michael McInerney
Dan Moore
Jason Morris
Julian Morris
Gary Platner
John Polidora
Eddie Rainwater
Glenn Rane
Dion Rogers
Danny Saint-Hilaire
Samwise
Robert Sevilla
John Scharmen
Gustav E Schmidt
Tiffany Sirignano
John Staats
Justin Thavirat
Rhett Torgoley
Wendy Vetter
Wei Wang
Holly Wilson
Thomas Yip
Jason Zirpolo

CINEMATIC ARTISTS
Brian Huang
Steve Hui
Bernie Kang
Graven Tung

BLIZZARD ENTERTAINMENT
Art Direction
Jeff Chamberlain
Glenn Rane
Chris Robinson

Creative Development Manager
Shawn Carnes
Creative Development Writer
Micky Neilson
Creative Development Editor
Evelyn Fredericksen
Creative Development Production
Evan Crawford
Stuart Massie
Gloria Soto
Director of Global Licensing
& Business Development
Cory Jones
Licensing Manager
Gina Pippin
WoW Team Production
J. Allen Brack
Rob Foote
Alex Mayberry
Additional Production
Randal Dumoret
Erik Jensen
Jeff Liu
Justin Parker
Special Thanks
Angela Blake

INSIGHT EDITIONS
Publisher & Creative Director
Raoul Goff
Project Manager
Jake Gerli
Art Director & Designer
Iain R. Morris
Production Manager
Leslie Cohen
Design Production Coordinator
Donna Lee

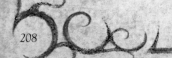